Sandwiches & Snacks

Susannah Blake

PowerKiDS
press.

New York

Published in 2009 by The Rosen Publishing Group Inc.
29 East 21st Street, New York, NY 10010

Copyright © 2009 Wayland/The Rosen Publishing Group, Inc.

First Edition

Senior editor: Jennifer Schofield
Designer: Jane Hawkins
Photographer: Andy Crawford
Proofreader: Susie Brooks

Library of Congress Cataloging-in-Publication Data

Blake, Susannah.
  Sandwiches and snacks / Susannah Blake. — 1st ed.
      p. cm. — (Make and eat)
  Includes index.
  ISBN 978-1-4358-2857-5 (lib. binding)
  ISBN 978-1-4358-2931-2 (paperback)
  ISBN 978-1-4358-2935-0 (6-pack)
  1. Sandwiches—Juvenile literature.
  2. Snack foods—Juvenile literature. I. Title.
  TX818.B53 2009
  641.8'4—dc22

                              2008025817

Manufactured in China

Acknowledgements:
The author and publisher would like to thank the following models: Adam Menditta, Jade Campbell, Demi Mensah, Robert Kilminster, Taylor Fulton, Kaine Zachary Levy, Ammar Duffus.

Web Sites

Due to the changing nature of Internet links, PowerKids Press has developed an online list of Web sites related to the subject of this book. This site is updated regularly. Please use this link to access this list: www.powerkidslinks.com/mae/ssnacks

Note to parents and teachers:

The recipes in this book are designed to be made by children. However, we recommend adult supervision at all times since the Publisher cannot be held responsible for any injury caused while making these recipes.

Contents

All about sandwiches and snacks   4

Creamy raita   6

Hummus wrap   8

Classic egg salad   10

Bruschetta   12

Quesadilla wedges   14

Chunky wedges and dip   16

Chicken pita pocket   18

Tuna melt   20

Glossary and Extra Information   22

Equipment   23

Index   24

All about sandwiches and snacks

Most sandwiches are made from two slices of bread with a filling spread in between. You can make all kinds of different sandwiches, depending on your choice of bread and filling. Snacks are usually smaller than a meal and can be anything from a crunchy apple to potato wedges and a dip. Snacks should be easy to make and just enough to fill a gap.

MAKING A SANDWICH

Choosing the bread for your sandwich is important, because the type of bread you choose will give the sandwich a particular taste and texture. Bread can be white or whole-wheat, or it can be made of rye, corn, or other grains. Shaped breads, such as a French baguette or a roll, are good for turning into chunky sandwiches. Pita breads can be split and the filling stuffed inside, and flatbreads, such as tortillas, can be rolled up around the filling to make a wrap.

You can put all kinds of filling inside your sandwich. They can be sweet or savory, and you can add just one filling or you might decide to have several. Popular fillings include peanut butter and jelly, cheese, ham, egg, tuna, chicken, and hummus. You can also add salad, such as sliced cucumber and tomato, alfalfa sprouts, lettuce, and coleslaw. You might also want to add extras, such as pickles, mustard, olive oil, and mayonnaise.

SIMPLE SNACKS

Different types of snacks are eaten all over the world. For example, if you lived in Italy, you may have some homemade bruschetta—tomato toasts—with some olives as an afternoon snack. If you lived in Mexico, nachos or quesadillas would be perfect to keep you going. Just like sandwiches, snacks can be sweet or spicy. Although snacks such as potato chips, cakes, and cookies are delicious, they are not very healthy and should be eaten only as a treat. Instead, snack on fruit and vegetables, such as oranges, bananas, and carrots.

GET STARTED!

In this book, you can learn to make a wide variety of sandwiches and snacks. All the recipes use everyday kitchen equipment, such as knives, spoons, forks, and cutting boards. You can see pictures of some of the different equipment that you may need on page 23. Before you start, check that you have all the equipment that you will need, and make a list of any ingredients that you need to buy. Make sure there is an adult to help you, especially with the recipes that involve using the stove or oven.

When you have everything you need, make sure all the kitchen surfaces are clean, and wash your hands well with soap and water. If you have long hair, tie it back. Always wash raw fruit and vegetables under cold running water before preparing or cooking them. This will help to remove any dirt and germs. Then, put on an apron and get cooking!

Creamy raita

This Indian dip is great for scooping up with poppadums. If you do not have poppadums, you could serve it with strips of red and orange peppers.

INGREDIENTS

For 4 servings:
- ½ large cucumber
- 1 cup Greek yogurt
- 1 garlic clove, peeled
- 2 tbsp fresh mint
- pinch of salt
- poppadums to serve

EXTRA EQUIPMENT
- sieve

1 Cut the cucumber in half lengthwise. Using a teaspoon, scrape out the seeds from each half and throw them away.

2 Grate each cucumber half. Be careful not to rub your fingers on the grater.

3 Put the cucumber in a sieve and hold it over the kitchen sink. Press down on the cucumber with your hand to squeeze out as much liquid as possible.

4 Put the cucumber in a medium-sized bowl and add the yogurt.

5 Crush the garlic in a garlic press and add it to the cucumber and yogurt.

6 To chop the mint, pluck off the leaves from the stems until you have a small handful of leaves. Roll the leaves into a loose ball and gently rock a knife over the leaves. Do this until the leaves are finely chopped.

7 Add the mint and a pinch of salt to the yogurt, and stir well. Taste the raita, and if necessary, add a pinch more salt and stir.

8 Put the minty raita into a serving bowl and serve with the poppadums.

MINTY CURES

Mint not only adds flavor to food, but it also has healing properties. Next time you have a stomachache, put some mint leaves in hot water. Leave the water to cool, then sip the minty tea.

Hummus wrap

A wrap is a kind of sandwich, but instead of putting the filling between two slices of bread, you roll it up inside a single flatbread. You can put all kinds of sandwich filling inside a wrap. When you have mastered this one, why not try another filling?

INGREDIENTS

For 1 serving:
- ¼ red pepper
- 1 tortilla
- 2 tbsp hummus
- handful of salad leaves

1 Put the pepper on the cutting board and gently pull out any seeds and leftover pith. Cut the pepper into small pieces and set them aside for later.

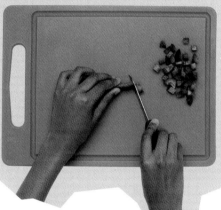

2 Put the tortilla on a board and spread the hummus over it.

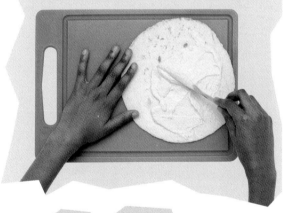

DELICIOUS HUMMUS

To make your own hummus, rinse and drain a can of chickpeas. Blend them with 1 crushed clove of garlic, 1 teaspoon of ground cumin, 1 teaspoon of ground coriander, 4 tablespoons of olive oil, 2 tablespoons of lemon juice, and 1 tablespoon of tahini (sesame seed paste).

3 Sprinkle the chopped pepper on across half of the tortilla.

4 Scatter the salad leaves on top of the chopped pepper.

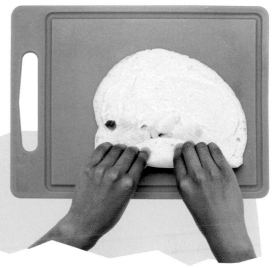

5 To roll up the tortilla, start rolling from the edge of the half that has the salad and peppers. Tuck in any stray leaves as you roll. The half of the tortilla that is covered with hummus, but has no chopped pepper or salad leaves, will help to stick the wrap together.

6 Cut the wrap in half across the middle to make two smaller wraps. Put them on a plate and serve.

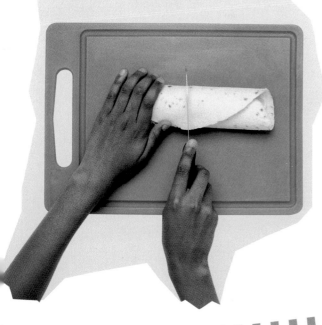

Classic egg salad

If you like this classic recipe, try putting a few slices of cucumber or tomato on top of the egg salad or adding a sprinkling of alfalfa sprouts. You could try using different types of bread, such as rye or a baguette, too.

INGREDIENTS

For 1 serving:
- 1 egg • water
- 1 tbsp mayonnaise
- 2 slices whole-grain bread
- salt and black pepper

Ask an adult to help you use the stove.

1 Put the egg in a small pan and pour in cold water to cover the egg by about 1½ in (4cm).

2 Bring the water to a boil—when you see bubbles, the water is boiling. Turn down the heat and let the water simmer gently for 10 minutes.

FRESH EGGS

As an egg gets older, the white and yolk start to change. If you compared a very fresh egg with a ten-day old egg and a 20-day old egg, you would see a big difference. The very fresh egg would have a fat, rounded yolk and two layers of white. As an egg gets older, the yolk becomes flatter and the difference between the two layers of white becomes less and less, until you can hardly notice it at all.

3 Turn off the heat and take the egg out of the water using a slotted spoon. Put the egg in a bowl of cold water and allow it to cool.

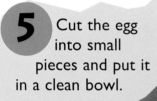**4** When the egg is cool, tap it against your work surface until the shell is cracked all over. Peel off the shell and rinse the egg under cold water to remove any leftover bits of shell.

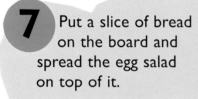**5** Cut the egg into small pieces and put it in a clean bowl.

6 Add the mayonnaise, a pinch of salt, and freshly ground black pepper to the egg and stir to mix.

7 Put a slice of bread on the board and spread the egg salad on top of it.

8 Place the second slice of bread on top and press down gently to make sure it is secure. Cut your sandwich in half from corner to corner to serve.

Bruschetta

Open sandwiches are ones that do not have a second slice of bread on top. *Bruschetta* are little Italian toasts that come somewhere between a mini-open sandwich and a snack.

INGREDIENTS

For 4 servings:
- 2 tomatoes
- 1¼ tsp olive oil
- 1 small baguette
- 1 garlic clove
- 8 fresh basil leaves
- salt and black pepper

Ask an adult to help you use the broiler.

1 Cut each tomato in half. Using your thumb, gently press out the seeds and jelly, and throw them away.

2 Finely chop the tomatoes and put them in a bowl. Sprinkle a pinch of salt and freshly ground black pepper on the tomatoes. Then pour 1 teaspoon of the olive oil on top, and stir gently. Set aside for later.

3 Wipe and dry the cutting board. Cut off the end of the baguette, then cut eight slices, about ¾ in. (2cm) thick.

4 Turn on the broiler. If it is an electric broiler, leave it to heat up for about 5 minutes. Place the bread slices on the rack and toast them so that both sides are golden.

5 Arrange the toasts on a serving plate. Cut the garlic clove in half, and rub the cut side over the top of each slice of toast. Garlic has a very strong taste, so you only need to rub the pieces gently to give them a good garlicky flavor.

6 Spoon the chopped tomatoes and any juices from the bowl on top of the toasts. Drizzle the rest of the olive oil over each of the toasts.

7 Top each of the toasts with a basil leaf before you serve the bruschetta.

ANTIPASTI

In Italy, little snacks, such as bruschetta, olives, marinated vegetables, and cold meats, are served as an appetizer before the main meal. These little snacks are called *antipasti*, which means "before the meal."

Quesadilla wedges

Quesadillas are a kind of fried sandwich from Mexico. This quesadilla is made with plain cheese, but in Mexico, chilies, vegetables, such as spinach and peppers, and ham are used to make quesadillas.

INGREDIENTS

For 4 servings:
- 2 oz. (60g) Cheddar cheese
- 2 plain tortillas
- ground black pepper

Ask an adult to help you use the stove.

1 Grate the cheese on a small plate. Be careful not to grate your fingers!

2 Heat a large nonstick frying pan over medium heat.

GRATE AWAY

The easiest way to grate cheese is to use a box-shaped cheese grater. Hold the grater firmly in one hand on a plate or board. Hold the block of cheese in the other hand and hold it against the top of the grater. Slide the cheese down against the teeth of the grater, and shreds of cheese will fall down inside the grater. Continue in the same way until you have grated enough cheese for your recipe.

3 Put a tortilla in the pan. Sprinkle the cheese on the tortilla in an even layer and grind some black pepper on top.

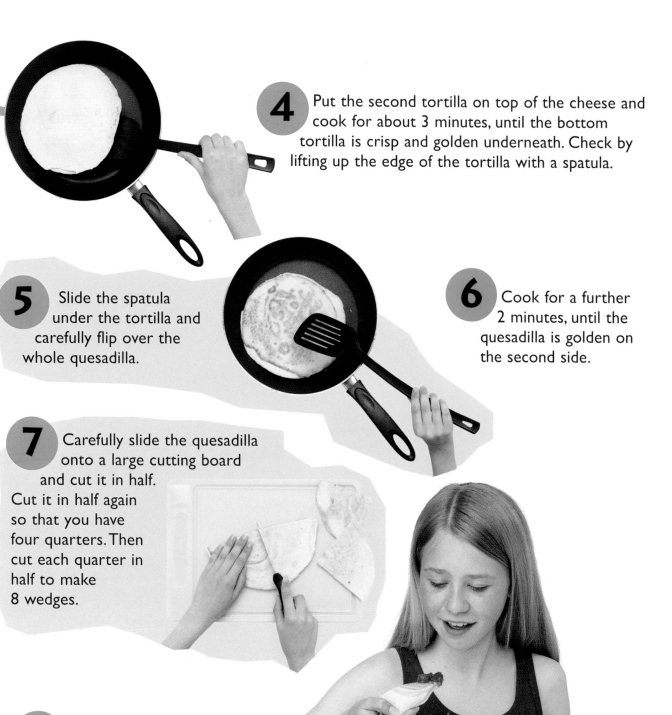

4 Put the second tortilla on top of the cheese and cook for about 3 minutes, until the bottom tortilla is crisp and golden underneath. Check by lifting up the edge of the tortilla with a spatula.

5 Slide the spatula under the tortilla and carefully flip over the whole quesadilla.

6 Cook for a further 2 minutes, until the quesadilla is golden on the second side.

7 Carefully slide the quesadilla onto a large cutting board and cut it in half. Cut it in half again so that you have four quarters. Then cut each quarter in half to make 8 wedges.

8 Pile the quesadilla wedges onto a plate and serve them right away, on their own or with some fresh salsa for dipping.

Chunky wedges and dip

These potato wedges make a really filling snack or a lunchtime treat. Be careful when you eat them, because they will be piping hot when you take them out of the oven!

INGREDIENTS

For 4 servings:
- 1 large potato, scrubbed and patted dry
- 1 tbsp olive oil
- salt and ground black pepper
- ½ cup natural yogurt
- 2 tsp pesto

Ask an adult to help you use the oven.

1 Preheat the oven to 375°F (190°C).

2 Cut the potato in half. Place the two halves on their flat sides and cut them into quarters. Cut each quarter into chunky wedges—like big steak fries.

POTATOES

Today, potatoes are eaten all over the world. However, this was not always the case. The very first potatoes were grown in South America, and there is evidence that they were eaten in Peru as far back as 2,000 years ago. Europeans first tasted potatoes in 1537 in what is now Colombia. In the 1550s, potatoes were brought to Spain and then, in 1590, to Britain.

3 Put the potato wedges in a roasting pan in a single layer. Brush with olive oil, then sprinkle a pinch of salt and grind some black pepper on top. Toss to coat the wedges so that they are glossy all over.

4 Bake the wedges for about 20 minutes. Wearing oven gloves, take the pan out of the oven and put it on a heatproof surface. Use a spatula to turn the wedges. Put the roasting pan back in the oven, and bake the wedges for another 15 minutes, until they are golden all over and tender.

5 Meanwhile, stir the yogurt and pesto together and spoon the dip into a serving bowl.

6 When the potatoes are golden, wearing oven gloves, remove the roasting pan from the oven and transfer wedges to a serving dish. Serve hot with the dip.

Chicken pita
pocket

You can buy precooked chicken breasts for this recipe—or you can ask an adult to broil a chicken breast for you. You could also use leftover cold roast chicken.

INGREDIENTS

For one serving:
- 1 carrot
- ½ broiled chicken breast
- ½ tsp sweet chili sauce
- 1 tsp olive oil
- ½ tsp white wine vinegar
- salt
- 1 pita bread
- small handful of salad leaves

Ask an adult to help you to use the broiler.

1 Cut off each end of the carrot. Using a vegetable peeler, peel off the skin.

2 Grate the carrot and put the grated pieces in a medium-sized bowl.

3 Put the chicken on the board and cut it into bite-sized pieces. Add it to the grated carrot.

4 To make the dressing, put the sweet chili sauce, olive oil, and vinegar in a small bowl. Add a pinch of salt and stir well.

5 Pour the dressing on the carrots and chicken, and mix it well.

6 Turn on the broiler. If you are using an electric broiler, leave it for about 5 minutes to heat it up. Put the pita bread under the broiler and warm it for a few minutes on each side until it starts to puff up.

7 Put the bread on the board—it will be full of hot steam that can burn, so be careful! Cut the bread in half and carefully open up the halves to make two pockets.

8 Put a couple of salad leaves in each pita pocket, then spoon the chicken and carrot salad on top. Eat warm or cold.

PITA BREAD

This soft, chewy flatbread is eaten all over the Middle East. It is made from wheat and is slightly leavened. When it is baked, the oval-shaped bread puffs up, leaving it hollow inside. This hollow makes a kind of pocket that makes pita bread perfect for stuffing to make a kind of sandwich.

Tuna melt

This is a classic open sandwich that is topped with tuna salad and melted cheese. Adding chopped gherkins to the tuna salad adds a tangy bite, but if you prefer to leave these out, the tuna also tastes great on its own.

INGREDIENTS

For 2 servings:

- 7 oz. (200g) can tuna, drained
- 2 gherkins or 1 large dill pickle (optional)
- 3 tbsp mayonnaise
- freshly ground black pepper
- 2 thick slices bread
- 2 large slices Jarlsberg or Swiss cheese, such as Emmental

Ask an adult to help you use the broiler.

1 Put the tuna in a bowl and break it up into flakes using a fork.

2 If you are using gherkins or a dill pickle, place on a board and chop finely. Add this to the tuna.

3 Add the mayonnaise and freshly ground black pepper to the tuna. Mix everything together.

4 Turn on the broiler. If you are using an electric broiler, leave it for about 5 minutes to heat up. Arrange the bread slices on the pan and place them under the broiler for a few minutes to toast one side.

5 Spread the untoasted side of bread with the tuna salad.

6 Top each slice of toast with a slice of cheese and then place the toast under the broiler until the cheese bubbles.

7 Carefully slide the toasts onto plates. You could serve the toast with a side salad of coleslaw.

HOLES IN CHEESE

Both Jarlsberg and Emmental cheese are made in similar ways and have the same kind of mild flavor. They are both full of holes, too. The holes appear when the cheese is made. Several bacteria are used to make the cheeses and as the cheeses mature, the bacteria produce carbon dioxide. This gas forms big bubbles in the cheese, which makes the holes.

Glossary

bacteria Invisibly small organisms that cannot been seen without a microscope. Some bacteria are good for us, but many, such as germs, can make us sick.

carbon dioxide A colorless gas. Carbon dioxide makes bubbles in certain types of cheese, and these bubbles make holes in the cheese.

filling The ingredients that go between the bread in a sandwich. Eggs, tuna, and cheese are all popular sandwich fillings.

hollow Empty.

leavened When dough has risen, it is leavened. Ingredients such as yeast and baking powder are known as leavening ingredients, because they cause dough to rise.

marinated When something is left to soak in a sauce. Oils and vinegars are often used as marinades.

Middle East The countries to the east of the Mediterranean Sea, from Egypt to Iran.

mild Not very strong. Jarlsberg cheese has a mild flavor.

poppadum An Indian flatbread that is thin and crispy. Poppadums are usually eaten with dips or chutneys.

rye A cereal used to make bread and crackers. Rye is similar in color to whole-wheat.

savory When flavors are tasty but not sweet. For example, cheese has a savory flavor.

tahini A savory dip that is made from sesame seeds. Tahini is usually used in Middle Eastern food.

texture The way the surface of something feels.

yolk The yellow of an egg.

BOOKS TO READ

Grilled Pizza Sandwich and Other Vegetarian Recipes
by Kristi Johnson (Capstone Press, 2008)

Kitchen for Kids
by Jennifer Low (Whitecap Books, 2004)

MEASUREMENT CONVERSIONS

Liquid
1 cup = 8 fl. oz. (250 ml)

Flour
1 cup = 4 oz. (115g)
1 tbsp = 1/2 oz. (15g)

Butter
1 stick = 4 oz. (115g)
1 tbsp = 1/2 oz. (15g)

Sugar
1 cup = 9 oz. (225g)
1 tbsp = 1 oz. (28g)

EXTRA INFORMATION

These abbreviations have been used:
• tbsp—tablespoon • tsp—teaspoon
• oz.—ounce • lb.—pound
• ml—millilitre • g—gram • l—litre

To work out where the stove dial needs to be for high, medium, and low heat, count the marks on the dial and divide it by three. The top few are high and the bottom few are low. The in-between ones are medium.

Equipment

MEASURING SPOONS

Measuring spoons help you to use the exact amount of ingredients.

SLOTTED SPOON

This spoon is useful for taking solid food out of liquids as the liquid drains through the holes.

MEASURING CUPS

These are used just like measuring spoons but for measuring bigger quantities of ingredients.

GARLIC PRESS

Crush garlic finely by putting a peeled garlic clove inside the press and squeezing the handle.

PASTRY BRUSH

Use to brush marinades and oil on foods.

CUTTING BOARDS

These protect your work surface. Make sure you keep your cutting boards clean, and always use a different one for meat and vegetables.

ROASTING PAN

Use this metal pan for roasting meat and vegetables in the oven.

KNIVES

Be careful when chopping and always keep your fingers away from the sharp blade.

FRYING PAN

Use this to fry food. You need to add very little butter or oil to a nonstick pan.

GRATER

Use to grate food such as cheese and carrots. Keep your fingers away from the sharp teeth of the grater.

Index

alfalfa sprouts 4, 10
antipasti 13
appetizers 13
apples 4

bacteria 21, 22
baguettes 4, 12
baking powder 22
bananas 5
basil 12
bread 4, 8, 10, 12, 20, 22
    see also types of bread
Britain 16
bruschetta 5, 12–13

carbon dioxide 21, 22
carrots 5, 18, 23
cheese 4, 14, 20, 21. 22
chicken 4, 18
    chicken pita pocket 18–19
chickpeas 8
chilies 14
chutney 4, 22
coleslaw 4
Colombia 16
coriander 8
cucumber 4, 6, 10
cumin 8
creamy raita 6–7

dill pickle 20
dips 4, 6, 16, 22
dough 22

eggs 4, 10, 22
    classic egg salad 10–11

fillings 4, 8, 22
flatbread 4, 8, 19, 22

garlic 6, 8, 12
gherkins 20
grains 4

ham 4, 14
hummus 4, 8

India 6
Italy 5, 12, 13

leavening 19, 22
lemon juice 8

mayonnaise 10, 20
Mexico 5, 14
Middle East 19, 22
mint 6, 7

nachos 5

olive oil 8
olives 5, 13
open sandwiches 12, 20
oranges 5

peppers 6, 8, 14
Peru 16
pesto 16
pickle 4
pita bread 4
popadums 6, 22

potatoes 16
    potato wedges 4, 16–17

quesadillas 5, 14
    quesadilla wedges 14–15

salad 4, 8, 18
South America 16
Spain 16
spinach 14
sweet chili sauce 18

tahini 8, 22
tomato 4, 5, 10, 12
tortilla 4, 8
tuna 4, 20, 22
    tuna melt 20–21

vinegar 18, 22

water 5, 7, 10
wheat 19
whole-grain bread 10
wraps 4, 8
    hummus wrap 8–9

yeast 22
yogurt 6, 16
yolk 10, 22